Friendship Matters

A Guide to Understanding Why Children
Have Trouble Making Friends and
What You Can Do About It.

ISA MARRS

Inquiries and requests for permission or further information
should be addressed to:
IMSLP, PC
127 Woodside Ave #201
Briarcliff Manor, NY 10510
Phone: (914) 488-5282

This publication is designed to provide accurate information
regarding the subject matter covered; however, the information
herein is provided as is and without any warranties either
expressed or implied. Facts and information contained in this
publication were believed to be accurate at the time they were
written and are to be used for informational purposes only. This
publication is not intended to replace medical, professional, or
other expert advice. If medical or other professional advice or
expert assistance is required, an appropriate and competent
professional person should be sought.

ISBN: 0692028102
ISBN-13: 9780692028100

IMSLP PC, Briarcliff Manor, NY

This book is dedicated to all the great kids I have worked with over the years and to the parents who love them.

ACKNOWLEDGMENTS

This was, in many ways, a group effort. This book would not have been possible without the inspiration and effort of my family, my team, and all the parents who have trusted me to help their children. Each of you has contributed in your own way. For that I sincerely thank you.

CONTENTS

Introduction

It is impossible to overstate the importance of friendships to children. Friendships play a vital role in their development.

SECTION I
Why Children Struggle to Fit In

Understanding why a child is struggling socially is the first step to helping.

CHAPTER 1
Us and Them

To its members the group represents "us," and everyone else is "them."
     Figure 1 Seven Signs Your Child Is Being Bullied

CHAPTER 2
Social Skills

Social-skills problems do not go away on their own. They become more pronounced

CHAPTER 7
Warning Signs

Social-skills deficits are much more common than most people think. Children who seem typical in every other way can have disordered social skills.
    Figure 3 The Most Important Social Milestones Your Child Should Be Reaching

Section II
What You Can Do at Home

While there is no way to replace the personalized guidance of a qualified professional, there are some things you can do at home that can be immensely helpful to your child.

CHAPTER 8
Friend-Away

There are some behaviors that repel friendships if not kept in check. Here are the eight most common friendship repellents and how you can help.

CHAPTER 9
Flexibility

Addressing mental and social flexibility is often a key to success when helping children with social-skills disorders.

ABOUT THE AUTHOR

Isa Marrs, MA, CCC-SLP, is a board-certified speech-language pathologist who specializes in pragmatic language (social-skills) disorders in children. She is an expert in the field who is frequently sought after by institutions and therapists to provide training for working with these and other disorders. Isa also served as a guest expert for Nickelodeon's ParentsConnect.com and has been quoted by numerous top media outlets, such as Disney's BabyZone.com, LoveToKnow.com, and Univision.

Isa has been helping children for more than twenty years. Her journey began while working with special-needs children as a teacher's aide at the age of fifteen. From that time she knew she wanted to work with children and help them reach their potential and has helped children and parents from impoverished rural areas of New Mexico all the way to super-affluent communities such as Westchester County, New York, and Greenwich, Connecticut. Some parents drive more than an hour each way, several times a week, to get her help for their children.

Isa lives in Westchester County with her husband, two wonderful children, and a menagerie of pets.

HER WEBSITES

Isa's websites, www.WhereICanBeMe.com and www.SpeechLanguageFeeding.com, are the go-to resources for parents and professionals. Stop by today and see why.

Introduction

*It is impossible to overstate the
importance of friendships to
children. Friendships play a vital
role in their development.*

Friendships matter. Our world is a social one, and to be successful in it, we must be able to form and maintain friendships. Our ability to do that as adults was formed by the relationships of our childhood. Our friends, acquaintances, and even enemies all taught us something about navigating the social world in which we live.

That is why it is impossible to overstate the importance of friendships to children. Friendships play a vital role in their development. Friendships give them a sense of security and belonging. Friendships teach them how to negotiate and compromise. Friendships teach them when to express their emotions and when not to. Friendships even teach children who they can trust and who they can't.

Friendships come naturally to most children. Most of them have the necessary skills to make new connections and build new relationships when they need to. Yet there are those children who just can't seem to make connections. They go through each day surrounded by other people and children, yet they are alone. While other children are laughing and playing together, they are left out. Sometimes they are merely overlooked. Other times they are treated with contempt. They always feel less than human when they are around other children. It is hard to imagine a worse feeling than that.

Why does this happen? It is not that these are bad kids. It's not that they don't deserve to have friends. It's not that they don't want friends. Most often they are great kids who want desperately for others to be friends with them. They want to be important to people other than their family members. They dream of feeling positive connections with people to whom they are not related. Unfortunately each day brings more disappointment. Through no fault of their own, they simply can't make and maintain friendships.

That's not to say they don't do the wrong things. They do. It may be they're too bossy, too emotional, too selfish, too grumpy, too perky, too quiet, too loud, too messy, too touchy, or too clueless. The lonely child may be a quitter, a liar, a gossiper, a talker who doesn't listen, or just plain weird. Really there are countless things some children do that make it hard if not impossible to be their friend. However, all of these outward behaviors are often symptoms of an underlying problem of which few professionals and even fewer parents are aware.

This lack of awareness leads to many of these children being labeled as behavior problems by teachers. While their behaviors may cause problems, rarely does anyone stop to ask what is causing the behaviors. How can we hope to change the behaviors if we don't address what is causing them?

Not addressing the problem is why so many of these children are falling through the cracks. It is why so many of them are struggling to find where they belong in the world. It is why so many of them feel like they are on the outside looking in—because they are. This is not a problem they can overcome on their own. They need help.

That is why I wrote this book—to help. By the time we are finished here, you will understand why your child is struggling socially and the steps you need to take to help. In short this is more than just a book; it is a tool you can use to help your child make friends and maintain relationships.

SECTION I

⤺⤻

Why Children Struggle to Fit In

⤺⤻

*Understanding why a child
is struggling socially is
the first step to helping.*

CHAPTER 1

Us and Them

To its members the group represents "us," and everyone else is "them."

By the age of one, babies recognize strangers and respond differently to them. It seems we are born with the instinct to separate people into groups of "us" and groups of "them." This segregating behavior gains momentum with each passing year. By the age of eight, children begin to form and join social cliques. When this happens you are either part of the clique, and you're one of *us*, or you're not part of the clique, and you're one of *them*.

It's no coincidence many parents start noticing that their children are falling behind socially at this age. This is when children are becoming more socially sophisticated and exclusionary at a very rapid pace. This behavior continues to gain momentum and then peaks during the teen years, when children are exerting independence from their parents. This is the age when the views of their peer groups become the driving forces behind their behavior.

Pay attention to groups of children at this age, and you'll see what I am talking about. Each group will have its own social norms. Each group will have members who dress alike, talk alike, act alike, and like to do the same things. To its members the group represents us, and everyone else is them.

Sometimes these groups get along; other times they don't. In some instances this behavior is akin to the warring tribes of our ancestors. The difference is kids today mostly use words and intellectual skills to fight for social position as opposed to spears and clubs to fight for territory. This behavior puts the children who do not belong to a group at a particular disadvantage. Groups provide protection. Not being part of a group greatly increases a child's risk of being targeted by bullies.

At its essence bullying is us and them behavior taken to the extreme. The main goal of all bullying is to establish and maintain dominance over the victim. What separates bullying from normal social sparring is intensity, frequency, and that the child being bullied does not have the ability to deal with the attacks effectively.

While most children are bullied at some point in their lives, most have enough social sophistication to fend off the attacks and reach us status with some group. They do this by decoding and following a set of rules that define the social behavior of the group that accepts them.

Every group has a set of rules that defines it. Being able to detect and follow those rules is critical to being a member of the group. These rules are mostly unspoken, but they do exist, and they are different from group to group.

The ability to set social rules and follow them is a survival strategy that has been with us since our ancestors first started organizing into groups. It is believed humans developed this ability because the group had to be cohesive in its thinking and behavior to survive.

Today we use this ability to determine who we can trust and who we cannot. Look around and you can see that this behavior remains a defining aspect of human nature. We see it in corporate culture. We see it in politics. We see it everywhere we look. Fairly or not your clothes, your car, your house, your mannerisms, and everything else about you symbolize the *us* you belong to. As neuroscientist Terence Deacon puts it, humans are the "symbolic species." We all do things to fit in and be part of the crowd. We may all do it with different things, but we all do it. Our natural tendency is to separate into groups of *us* and *them*.

Our ability to adapt and fit in with these different groups is determined by something called *social skills*. When someone lacks social skills, he or she cannot adapt to become an us. These skills are essential to making and maintaining friendships. However, our social skills affect much more than friendships. They affect our ability to function in our daily lives. In order to be independent, we must be able to navigate through social situations.

It's no secret employers look not only at your technical skills but also how you will fit in to their culture when you are being interviewed. They know your social ability, or *interpersonal skills,* as they call it, is at least as important if not more important than your technical skills. It's much easier to teach a technical skill than it is to change a behavior or improve someone's social skills. While both are important, the ability to adapt to different social environments is more important to our future success than anything we learn in academics. The more connected we become as a species, the more true this will be.

Our social skills determine our ability to navigate all situations that involve more than one person. Social skills are even playing a role in my writing this. As I write I must consider your perspective. Will you enjoy what I write? Will you get the point I'm trying to make, or will you infer something else altogether? Will you find what I say offensive? For me to answer those questions while writing, I must draw on past social experiences to take your perspective.

The ability to take someone else's perspective and anticipate his or her response is a component of something called *perspective taking*. Most people have this skill. Perspective taking is what gives us the ability to empathize with others and to see their points of view. For example, if you and I were speaking, I would be able to judge your reaction by your tone of voice, your posture, and any number of other social cues. I could then modify what I was saying based on your response. It might involve taking the subject further or dropping it altogether if I see it upsets you. In other words by taking your perspective, I am able to know if I am violating your social rules or not. In turn you are deciding whether or not I have. If I have not violated your social rules, and you have not violated mine, then our relationship will continue.

Everyone is constantly making these judgments with the people they meet. Everyone is deciding who belongs with us and who belongs with them. We cannot escape this. It is human nature. Therein is the importance of having effective social skills. They are what give us the ability to become part of an us.

FIGURE 1

Seven Signs Your Child Is Being Bullied

1. **Change in behavior or mood.** Children may become withdrawn, anxious, angry, sad, and/or less confident.

2. **Decrease in appetite.** A child may sit at the table and not eat.

3. **Frequent missing or broken possessions.** Clothes may be torn, lunch money may be stolen, or books may be destroyed.

4. **Difficulty sleeping and nightmares.**

5. **Always looking for a new way to get to school.**

6. **Sudden change in grades.** A child may start to do poorly in a subject he or she has always done well in with no explanation.

7. **Starts coming up with every excuse not to go to school.**

CHAPTER 2

Social Skills

---

*Social-skills problems do not go
away on their own. They become
more pronounced and habitual
because social situations become
more complex as time goes on.*

Social-skills difficulties sneak up on most parents.
Suddenly the child who played alongside the other kids
is feeling isolated and unable to make friends. This happens
because of how quickly social interactions change once a
child moves out of toddlerhood. While being able to take
turns was once enough, now the child must be able to grasp
the nuances of both verbal and nonverbal language. He or
she must also be able to distinguish between literal and non-
literal language. And while we take it for granted, this is not
an easy thing to do.

The worst part of the whole thing is that with only a few
specific exceptions, these children want to make friends.
They just don't know how to do so. Parents often tell me it

is hard to understand why their child "just doesn't get it." One reason is because their child is unable to learn social skills through experience like other children. Instead he or she must be taught.

Not knowing this, many parents get frustrated when they see their child struggle in settings with children who have good social skills. Often they have put their child in these settings because they hope he or she will learn from the other children. The parents do not realize their child is unable to pick up on social cues and learn them like most other children. While these social environments are important to practice new skills, it is not the place to learn social skills. Everything moves too quickly, and it sets the child up for failure.

Putting children in environments with others who are more socially sophisticated also risks their being misunderstood by the other children and adults, which leads to their being labeled as the weird, mean, or bad kid. Sometimes they're simply labeled as troublemakers. This is common within structured settings, such as schools. Many children who receive these negative labels are actually suffering from a social-skills disorder. It isn't that they are bad kids; it's that they don't really understand what they are doing wrong or what they are supposed to do in a given situation.

For example, a child who's overly blunt may be prone to hurting other children's feelings without meaning to. Even though children like this do not understand what they are doing wrong, they may get in trouble. The same goes for the child who is prone to saying inappropriate things, talking out of order, or hiding under the desk. Really there are countless things that may get a child labeled as a behavior problem when in reality he or she is suffering from a social-skills disorder.

Unfortunately, when children are given these negative labels, they often feel it is their responsibility to live up to them. There is a little boy I know well who I will call Brian (not his real name). He is an active boy with some attention and sensory issues. Brian is also a very bright boy who doesn't miss a thing. One day when he was doing something he should not have been doing, I asked him why he was doing it. He replied, "Because I am Brian." I shared this comment with his parents, who now work hard at avoiding negative labels. However, while we can control the labels given to our children in our own homes, we cannot control how they are labeled outside our homes.

Social-skills problems do not go away on their own. They typically become more pronounced and habitual because social situations become more complex as time goes on. To put that another way, the social requirements are much different for a five-year-old than they are for a thirteen-year-old.

As time goes on, these social struggles become more difficult and frustrating for parents and children. A mom at a health fair told me her son said, "Mom, I always feel like there is something I am missing, and I just don't know what it is."

Another mom from New York said to me, "My daughter is going into third grade, and she still does not have one friend. She has been in the same school since kindergarten... All I want is for her to have at least one friend so she does not hate school, and she is not so lonely."

A mom from Connecticut told me, "Kids make fun of him, even going so far as to call him weird and telling him to get away from them. It hurts his feelings, and I can't really do anything about it."

A mom from Worthington, United Kingdom, told me her child who struggles socially is "being led into bad situations by others at school unknowingly."

A mom from Nevada contacted me and said her "very smart eleven-year-old daughter loves school"; however, "she has kids she knows and will talk to but no real friends. She cries at night and doesn't want to go to recess or lunch at school."

The best thing to do is to work on these skills early, before your child becomes too aware of what is happening and before bad habits begin to develop. This will help your child effectively interact with his or her peers. Whatever you do, do not push these needs aside until they become overly apparent. Every day I hear from parents of older children, teens, and young adults who are full of regrets from waiting.

For example, a Westchester mom of a young adult said to me, "I wish I could put my oldest son in one of your groups. I am really concerned about him. He struggles with social issues and fitting in. It may be that he's not able to put himself in the other person's shoes and generally has negative things to say. He has a few friends, but they always seem to cancel on him. I guess I always knew something was going on, but I didn't know what to do."

I wish I could say such stories are uncommon, but they are not. I hear stories like this every day. For more than twenty years, I have worked with children who have these challenges in their lives. All children want to fit in, and all parents want their child to have friends. We are social beings by nature, and we suffer when we don't have other people on whom we can depend. This gets exacerbated in social situations such as school. This is why children who have trouble socially are at greater risk of suffering from anxiety, depression, substance abuse, and social isolation.

These children are also at greater risk of being bullied since they are unable to pick up on and follow the social rules that would allow them to become part of a group. Bullying can significantly exacerbate a child's social problems. It can make a child less likely to be accepted by other peers since it becomes more socially risky to accept the bullied child into the group. It can also cause a child to adopt negative skills that make him or her more of a target.

Children who do not have the skills to escape bullying tend to adopt a strategy of avoidance. They see threats where they don't exist and increasingly isolate themselves. They also exhibit nervousness and timidity by constantly being on the lookout for signs of an attack. This behavior sends signals to bullies that they are easy targets. So the cycle feeds itself. As the children behave more like victims, other children treat them as victims, which makes the children act more like victims. The children who get stuck in this cycle grow up to be the adults who always seem to have bad things happen to them. A large part of this stems from patterns of behavior and expectations that have been with them since the early days, when they started to fail socially.

Unfortunately research shows that few of these children are getting the help they need. There is a profound lack of awareness and understanding of this problem within our health and education systems. Even when there is awareness, the vast majority of the efforts to help these children fail.

The consequences of this are devastating and long lasting. As I said before, social-skills problems do not go away on their own. It takes a great deal of time, effort, and know-how to help these kids. We'll talk more about that in later chapters; for now there is a lot more you need to know about social skills.

FIGURE 2

What Substantially Increases the Risk of a Child Having a Social-Skills Disorder?

Learning disorders: Studies show that on average 75 percent of children with learning disorders will have problems with social skills. When children have trouble learning in one area, they typically have trouble learning in other areas.

Language disorders: While often considered learning disorders, language disorders deserve a special place on this list since social skills are pragmatic language. Children having trouble with expressive or receptive language will also have trouble developing appropriate social skills. Children who have trouble with language or speech are also more likely to be excluded from peer groups and targeted by bullies.

ADHD: Studies show that children with ADHD are approximately 400 percent more likely to be rejected by peers than non-ADHD children, with as many as half of all children with ADHD suffering from rejection by their peers. It is worth noting that some research indicates preteen girls with ADHD are more likely to be rejected or bullied by their peers than are boys with ADHD.

Autism-spectrum disorders: The inability to connect socially with others is a defining characteristic of autism spectrum disorders including Asperger's syndrome. There is a direct correlation between the severity of the disorder and the impact of the child's social skills. While not all children who have social-skills disorders are on the autistic spectrum, all children on the autistic spectrum have social-skills disorders.

*Please note this list is not exhaustive. Many other special-needs classifications increase risk of social failure. This list represents some of the most common risk factors.

CHAPTER 3

Boys versus Girls

Men and women generally differ greatly in how they express their emotions and deal with their problems. We start to see these differences in early childhood.

When my son was first born, I was often asked if I felt or acted any differently with my boy than with my girl. Of course if you have a boy and a girl then you know the answer to this question is, "Absolutely not"—at least not at first. To me, when they were newborns, there was no difference. My little guy was a lot calmer than my daughter was as a baby; however, that was just personality.

This question got me thinking more about the differences between boys and girls, especially when it comes to language and social development. Interestingly, despite stories to the contrary, boys hit all major motor milestones about the same time as girls according to research. This includes milestones such as crawling and walking. However, during the preschool years, boys surpass girls in their motor skills pretty consistently.

When it comes to language development, girls talk sooner and understand language better at twelve months than boys do. At sixteen months girls will use an average of one hundred words compared to thirty words used by boys of the same age. That's a pretty big difference; however, this difference will decrease quickly. Boys catch up by age two and a half. At this age both boys and girls use about five hundred words when there are no delays.

A real difference between boys and girls is seen in their social skills. Boys tend to be more direct while girls tend to think more about the feelings of others. For example, Campbell Leaper, a professor of psychology at the University Of California, conducted an experiment in which boys and girls were given salted lemonade that tasted terrible. When asked about the taste, the girls tended to put on happy faces and say the lemonade tasted good. The boys were much more likely to say how bad it was and make a pretty big deal out of it.

While there are some real differences in how male and female brains develop and function, it is thought that these reactions have more to do with societal norms than they do with actual biological differences. Even if a set of parents treats their son and daughter the same, and even if they play the same games and encourage the same behaviors, society does not. Unless you live in a bubble, everywhere you look you can see differences in male and female roles. This plays a significant role in our children's identities and social behavior.

There are also some biological differences that contribute to the social differences of boys and girls. Sex hormones begin to affect development in utero and will continue to influence gender differences throughout development. Differences in nerve tissue that connects the hemispheres of the brain can be detected as early as twenty-six weeks' gestation. This tissue is thicker for baby girls than it is for boys. As adults the brains of women have more white matter while male brains have more gray matter. White matter connects different parts of the brain while gray matter is associated with thinking. This could explain some of the differences in behavior, perception, and technical skills between the genders.

Whatever the reason, these differences do exist, and they are thought to be major contributors to why boys are being diagnosed with ADHD and failing in school at much higher rates than girls. Our society is evolving to favor feminine traits, such as being able to talk, look, and listen. Boys like to move, do, and multitask. Unfortunately for them our schools are no longer set up to meet their social needs. Recess and other outlets for boys to release their energy are being cut back. Boys are being asked to sit still and listen, which, on average, is much harder for them to do than it is for girls. Unfortunately the difficulties for boys do not stop upon graduation.

Today's economy is increasingly rewarding social skills that have traditionally been considered feminine. In fact, as of 2009, the workforce became dominated by women for the first time in American history. There are also more women going to college and starting businesses while more men are dropping out of school, losing their jobs, and moving back in with their parents. This is happening because many boys and men are not adapting to the current social environment. They are not adjusting their behavior to fit in, and as a result they are being left behind.

As parents, therapists, and educators, we need to be aware of these social differences between boys and girls so we can better help them adapt to the changing social world around them. Regardless of whether they are boys or girls, we have to help our children learn to decode the unwritten social rules of life.

CHAPTER 4

Hidden Rules

The hidden curriculum is made up of rules that are not directly taught but every person is expected to know.

How many times have you done something embarrassing? Well, you're not alone. We all embarrass ourselves sometimes. Most often it's because we've violated some unwritten rule. These unwritten rules are what dictate our social interactions. They vary depending on where you live, your age, and your gender, among other things. They are generally unstated. However, they do exist, and they dictate our behavior.

We all try to follow these rules. Some of us are much better at recognizing and adapting to them than others are.

The ability to recognize and follow these hidden rules typically begins between the ages of five and seven. At these ages children will change their behaviors to fit in with those around them. This is also when it starts to become apparent that one child does not know the rules. This is especially true with girls.

Parents of girls often tell me stories of watching their daughters on the outside of social cliques during parties. They are often surprised at how socially sophisticated the other girls are.

Between the ages of five and seven, children should have the natural ability to pick up on social cues and be able to adjust their behaviors to match the situation. When they do not have the ability to pick up on social cues, they will continue to break the rules and fall further behind socially.

We've all been in situations where we didn't know the rules. It's no fun. You know the feeling: Your mouth gets dry. You start to sweat. Maybe you even get a little flushed. That's because you don't know the code.

When we don't know the code, most of us try to take our cues from those around us. We assume they know what to do, and if we just do what they do, we won't do something wrong and make a bad first impression.

Pay attention to your own actions throughout the day. Consider how differently you talk to the people you encounter. Everyone acts differently with their friends than they do with strangers, coworkers, and clients. Listen to your spouse the next time he or she is on the phone. Can you tell if the person on the line is a friend by how your spouse talks? I know I can tell when my husband, Jason, is talking with someone from New Mexico because his Southern drawl becomes more pronounced. My daughter does the same thing when she talks to Jason's family. She does their accent so well, they don't even notice. We do because we hear her switch back and forth.

There is actually a name for this. It's called *code switching*. While it does not always involve picking up someone's accent, it does require using the other person's social language. People who can master this are often better liked as they can adapt according to who they are talking to. It makes people feel safe and comfortable when you can speak their "language." When you can't it makes them and you uncomfortable. To speak someone else's language, you must be able to decode something called the *hidden curriculum*.

HOW THE HIDDEN CURRICULUM IS AFFECTING YOUR CHILD

Quite often I find myself explaining to parents why their child is having such difficulty making friends. They come to me with the knowledge that their child struggles in this area; however, it seems really to be an eye-opener when I explain why the child is having trouble and what is actually getting in the child's way.

To do this I go through an informal interview I have developed that assesses a child's social ability. One of the many things I look at is how well the child understands the hidden curriculum, which is made up of rules that are not directly taught but every person is expected to know. While most people don't even realize these unwritten rules exist, it is extremely obvious to most of us when one of them gets broken.

For example, think about how you would feel if you were alone on an elevator and a stranger got on and stood next to you instead of standing on the opposite side. If you are like most people, that would make you feel very uncomfortable, and you would likely try to move away. If that stranger understood the hidden curriculum and had just made a mistake, he would pick up on your social cue and move away as well. If he didn't understand the hidden curriculum, he might move closer to you.

Quite often, misunderstanding rules comes across as misbehaving and being rude. I am sure you can see how this is possible. However, when people have social-skills disorders, they do not intend to be rude; they just do not know the rules in a given situation. This causes a great deal of anxiety for them because they know something is expected of them—they just don't know what it is.

In each new social situation, the rules change. Each of us has somewhat different rules we want others to follow when they interact with us, and when people understand the hidden curriculum, they are able to pick up on the cues and adjust their behaviors as necessary. This allows them to speak our language.

For those who don't have that ability to decode the hidden curriculum, it's a little like starting a new job and not having a clue about what is supposed to be done; they feel awkward, uncomfortable, and out of place. The difference is that when people are unable to decode the hidden curriculum, they feel that way all the time. For such people the social rules are a mystery they can't figure out on their own.

Unfortunately many parents and professionals don't understand why this is happening. I find that knowing why something is or is not happening can be somewhat comforting. It helps us understand how to move forward. Once we identify why something is happening, we can treat it. Treatment is crucial to helping these individuals reach their potential.

That being said, there will always be another unwritten rule lurking behind the door in every different situation.

Social rules evolve. Something that was perfectly acceptable five years ago may not be acceptable today and vice versa.

We are social beings whose interactions are becoming progressively more complex. Not only do we need to understand the rules for in-person interactions, but we must also understand how they differ from managing social relationships across multiple digital platforms and multiple cultures.

For children who struggle with learning the hidden curriculum, social situations will always be more challenging than they are for children with typical social skills. That doesn't mean they'll never fit in. It just means they need help understanding how to make their way, and we need to help others understand them so they will be more accepted.

CHAPTER 5

Mind Blind

It is extremely difficult for those who have trouble with theory of mind to form relationships with people outside their families.

Have you ever looked at someone and known exactly what he or she was thinking? Many people experience this with best friends and siblings. Something happens, they look at their friends, and they just know exactly what is going through their minds. It's almost like mind reading.

What you may not realize is that most people are able to do this to some degree with everyone they meet. You may not know exactly what the other person is thinking, but you are able to develop a general idea. You know the person may want out of the conversation if he or she is looking around and checking the time. You know if you see tears in someone's eyes, the person is upset. Each of us is able to do this because of *perspective taking*. That is how we relate to others. We are able to perceive someone else's thoughts, feelings, and motivations. In other words it is the ability to see things from someone else's perspective and empathize with that person.

A necessary component of perspective taking is something called *theory of mind*. That refers to our ability not only to understand that people have different beliefs, motivations, knowledge, and moods but also to understand how these differences affect their actions and behaviors as well as our own. When people lack theory of mind, they are considered to have *mind blindness*.

Children who are developing typically will have theory of mind by three to four years of age. Their use of and dependence on it will continue to develop as they get older and social demands increase. While some parents may suspect their child is different from other children during this age range, most don't begin to get alarmed until social cliques start to form around age eight. To be part of a social group, a child must be able to follow the rules of that group. Children who have trouble with theory of mind and perspective taking will struggle to keep up with the rapidly changing social sophistication of other children. Unfortunately these children are often blamed for their lack of social ability because they can seem normal, even gifted, in every other way.

Parents, teachers, and especially other children tend to think these children are being intentionally weird, stubborn, or selfish. They do not realize these children simply do not have the ability to take other people's perspectives and understand their motivations, actions, and behaviors. The ability to see things from someone else's perspective is an essential skill for being able to share and resolve conflicts appropriately. That is why it is extremely difficult for those who have trouble with theory of mind and perspective taking to form relationships with people outside their families.

THE DIFFICULT TASK OF DETECTION

Recognizing that a child has trouble with theory of mind and perspective taking is not easy. Most professionals do not even know what these deficits, are let alone how to identify them accurately. That is why I often call social-skills deficits, and especially their underlying causes, the most subtle and profound deficits a child can have. These deficits are typically misdiagnosed as some form of behavior problem. So as you read these examples, please keep in mind that only those with significant deficits are easy to describe in writing. These deficits can be much more subtle than this.

One of the original and most well-known tests is called the *Smarties test*. In the original test, children who were developing typically were tested against children with autism. Both groups were shown a package with a Smarties label on it. When the children were asked what was in the container, they all answered "Smarties." They were then shown that the container actually had pencils in it.

Each group was then asked what the next group of children would think was in the package when they came in the room. The typically developing children all answered "Smarties." The children with autism answered "pencils." This happened because the typically developing children understood that the next person coming in would judge the contents of the box by the label. The children with autism were unable to do that because they did not have theory of mind.

In my social-skills classes, I often do an activity I call the *gift test* in which the children decide what gifts would be appropriate or inappropriate for their peers, family members, and other people in general. This activity shows who has difficulty with theory of mind and perspective taking. In one class of five young children, the deficit was clearly evident in one of them. I went around the table and asked all the children what they would buy for their parents, grandparents, and even a baby for the holidays. The one little girl who did not have theory of mind answered a Barbie doll for everyone. It was clear this was what she wanted for a holiday gift. She wanted it, so she believed other people would want it too. She was unable to get inside others' thoughts and decide what might be good gifts for them.

READING BETWEEN THE LINES

It is important to remember that things that are obvious to most of us are not obvious to a child who has trouble with theory of mind and perspective taking. Many of these children take things very literally. They struggle with reading between the lines to understand the implied meaning. For example, one child I work with is a teenager I'll call Abby (not her real name). She struggles socially. She also has trouble with theory of mind and perspective taking.

One day Abby got invited to a new friend's house for a school project. Her parents agreed she could go but insisted she call them when she got to the friend's house. Unfortunately the friend's mom needed to run some errands to get the materials for their school project. As time passed, Abby's parents grew more and more concerned. They knew she should have been at the friend's house within fifteen minutes of leaving school. So after an hour they called Abby on her cell phone and were very upset.

Abby became upset that they were upset because she felt she hadn't done anything wrong. She had planned to do as they had asked. She was going to call when she got to the friend's house, and they were not there yet. What she did not understand was her parents' implied meaning. Her parents really wanted a timely update to let them know she was okay. They also wanted to know if there were any changes to the plan. Abby had missed this implied meaning because she could not take their perspective. She failed to read between the lines.

Many of the things people say mean something more or even different from what is verbally stated. For example, I may look at the table and tell one of my children or my husband, "That's a really big mess you made." They all know that means I want the mess cleaned up. If they had trouble with theory of mind or perspective taking, they might think I was just making an observation. The same goes for statements such as, "You left the light on in the bathroom again" or "You're awfully quiet tonight." Everyone makes these sorts of statements that mean a great deal more than what is stated.

There also are many different questions that are not meant to be taken literally. For example, "What's up?" is not asking what is up above your head, and "Does my butt look big in these jeans?" is not expected to get a yes even if it's the honest answer.

Most people have the ability to recognize these things intuitively even without experience. They judge the tone of voice. They analyze the body language, and they consider the context, along with a whole host of other factors within a split second. They are able to take the other person's perspective and interpret the unstated meanings. It is a gift most of us take for granted.

MONKEY SEE, MONKEY DO: WHAT MIRROR NEURONS HAVE TO DO WITH IT

Have you ever wondered why you cringe at the pain of seeing someone get hurt or why you feel the agony of the parents who have lost their child when you've only seen them talking about it on the news? This response to others is at the root of being human. While it may not be as intense, we have the ability to feel what others feel without actually going through what they are going through.

By nature we are all copycats. We like to think of ourselves as being rugged individuals, but the reality is that when we are around others, we take on their behaviors. We code switch to reflect how they speak and how they move their bodies. We feel what they feel. They do the same thing. This subconscious action is called *mirroring*. The more time we spend together, the better we become at doing this, and the more in sync we become.

Studies show we unconsciously judge other people by their ability to mirror. We like them better when they mirror us, and they like us better when we mirror them. That is what is happening when we have a connection; we see someone else who is like us.

Some scientists believe this is caused by something called a *mirror neuron*. Without our knowledge these little neurons are lighting up like little Christmas trees as we go about our days. Brain scans show that even something as simple as watching another person reach for a pencil will cause our mirror neurons to fire. This is believed to be how we understand the motives of others. Because of mirror neurons, we literally experience what others are experiencing.

The research on this topic is compelling, and the implications are profound. It explains why there are proven relationships between what children view on television and how they behave. It explains why it is so difficult to change a behavior, such as drug addiction, without changing friends.

When our minds witness something, we experience it even though we are not participating in it. While we may not experience it with quite the same intensity, we feel the rush. We feel the passion. We feel the pain or whatever else may be going on around us. This is what gives us the ability to take the perspective of others and understand what is going on in their minds.

While the research into mirror neurons is new and far from complete, the understanding that we mirror others is not. Our ability to mirror others is critical to our ability to navigate the social world. Our ability to imitate others plays an important role in our lives and how we develop. This is why the behavior you model for your children is so important. This is also why peer groups have such big influences on children and why proper placement is so critical to your child's success in school or a social-skills program.

As I noted before, humans are copycats. Both consciously and unconsciously, we imitate those around us. This is how we decode the hidden curriculum and detect all the different social rules we follow each day. When children have trouble with perspective taking and theory of mind, they are not able to do this effectively on their own. They need outside help.

CHAPTER 6

Language

Our voices, the rates of our speech, our movements, and even the amounts of space we keep between ourselves and others send social signals to those around us.

Many parents are stunned to find out language and not behavior is the root cause of social-skills problems. This is even the case for children who are considered to be great talkers and of gifted intelligence. This comes as a surprise because they are unaware of something called *pragmatic language*, which is how we interpret and express the hidden curriculum. It is the social use of language. Any time there is more than one person, pragmatic language is being used.

It is important to understand that pragmatic language is not the same as being able to speak fluently, use big words, or speak in depth on topics of interest. Pragmatic language is more than just the words you use. It is the tone of your voice, the rate of your speech, your movements, your conversational turn-taking, and even the amount of space you keep between yourself and others. Everything you do in the presence of others sends social signals and is considered pragmatic language. In fact as strange as it may sound, we do not need to say anything verbally to use pragmatic language. That is because so much of what we say is communicated through our body language.

Think back to the example I gave in chapter 4 of the stranger crowding your space in the elevator. When you step away from the stranger, you are using nonverbal communication to let him know he is making you uncomfortable. If he takes a step toward you when you step back, he has violated the statement you just communicated nonverbally. Without knowing the stranger's intent, you may find his move toward you threatening. At the very least, you would find it annoying. On the other hand, if the stranger stays in place when you step away, you will likely feel less bothered by his presence. And if he were to take a step back after seeing you step back, he would be giving you a nonverbal apology for crowding your space.

Without giving it much if any thought, we all participate in nonverbal dances with those around us. We use almost all areas of our bodies to communicate messages. We step back to tell others they are too close. We step forward to say we want to be closer. We may cross our arms and shake our heads to show disappointment or flail our arms around to show excitement. There are countless nonverbal signals we are constantly sending to other people.

The next time you are around a group of people, watch how they interact with their bodies. You'll be able to get a good idea of the types of conversations they are having just by watching their movements and expressions. You'll know if they are happy conversations or stressful ones. You'll know if one of them is flirting. You'll even be able to determine who the leader is just by watching how the group members interact even. You don't need to hear a word they say to figure all of this out.

It is widely agreed that 60 to 90 percent of our communication is nonverbal. Some experts say as much as 97 percent of our communication is nonverbal. Before a word is ever uttered, we use strangers' clothing, facial expressions, postures, and a whole host of other nonverbal cues to judge them. For the most part, it is all done unconsciously, but it is done.

Now, before you try to tell me that you would never do such a thing, consider this: Do you judge people as being more or less honest when they don't make eye contact with you? We've all been taught that less eye contact equals less honest.

As the old saying goes, the eyes are the windows to the soul. But again how we use our eyes is only a small part of nonverbal communication. It's a mistake to think nonverbal communication is only body language.

The way we use our voices is another very important component of nonverbal communication. The way we change our rates, rhythms, volumes, and tones of voice is something called *prosody*. It is how we convey the emotion of our words, and it makes a huge difference in how a message is received.

Consider the differences between some of our past presidents when they spoke. Specifically think about Reagan, Clinton, and Obama versus George W. Bush. What immediately comes to your mind? Regardless of your politics, I'm sure we can agree the first three are much better speakers than President Bush was. The media and the public spent a great deal of time mocking him and questioning his intelligence because of the way he spoke. If we were to have each of these presidents deliver the same message to an audience that had never heard of them, the first three would connect with far more people than the last one. They would be judged as more intelligent not because of what they said but because of how they said it.

How something is said matters as much or more than what is actually said. This is considered *expressive nonverbal communication*. Of course we must not only be able to use all these nonverbal cues to express ourselves, but we must also be able to interpret them. That's called *receptive nonverbal communication*.

NVLD: THE QUIET DEVELOPMENTAL DISORDER

While most of us are able to pick up on nonverbal social rules without being formally taught, many can't. They have something psychologists call dyssemia. This is the social-dysfunction aspect of a nonverbal learning disorder (NVLD).

NVLD is sometimes known as *the quiet developmental disorder*. Parents of children with NVLD will often say they always felt something was not right; however, no one was able to put a finger on exactly what was wrong. There are several red flags when children have an NVLD, such as motor delays and visual-spatial difficulties. These children will also talk a lot but seem to say nothing. They have difficulty getting the main idea or the big picture.

As you can imagine, these disorders are easy for most people to miss. It doesn't matter if it is verbal, nonverbal, or both, children with any form of pragmatic language disorder typically go unnoticed until they fall far behind their peers. Even then they may get dismissed as just being weird or as someone who just doesn't get it. Many times they are even blamed for their behaviors because people think they are intentionally being difficult to get along with. These are some of the reasons why so many of these kids fall through the cracks and become adults who struggle socially. It is also why they are prone to suffer from anxiety and depression.

Most people, and especially children, want to get along with others. They may develop defensive behaviors that make it seem otherwise, but they do want to have friends. They just don't have the necessary skills to start and maintain relationships.

CHAPTER 7

Warning Signs

Social-skills deficits are much more common than most people think. Children who seem typical in every other way can have disordered social skills.

Social-skills deficits are the most subtle and profound deficits a child can have. Everything else can be perfectly normal. A child can be good looking and intelligent, with a strong command of language, and still be lost socially. It is no wonder these disorders are wildly misunderstood and misdiagnosed—few parents or professionals know how to recognize them. That is why this chapter is dedicated to changing that. We'll start with the seven warning signs of a social-skills disorder and end with the most important social milestones that children should reach between the ages of one and fourteen.

THE SEVEN CRITICAL WARNING SIGNS

Warning Sign #1: Not Having Friends Is a Biggie

That's the number-one reason I hear from parents, and for most children this matters a lot. The vast majority of kids do want friends, even if they think of themselves as being loners. While there are some children on the autistic spectrum who genuinely don't seem to want friends, all other children do. Even when children really don't want friends, it is important for them to have the skills to develop and manage relationships because they are a fact of life in our world. Humans are social creatures, and one of the biggest predictors of personal and/or financial success is having good social skills.

Warning Sign #2: Not Able to Keep Friends

Some kids are able to make friends, but they just can't keep them. This often has to do with a lack of flexibility, but there are other social skills that can contribute to this as well.

Warning Sign #3: Gets Bullied

While most children suffer some amount of bullying at some point in their lives, children with poor social skills are much more likely to be bullied. They make easy targets because they tend to act differently from other children and do not have the social skills to defend themselves.

Warning Sign #4: Doesn't Notice When Others Are Bored with the Conversation

Some kids can go on and on and on about things that interest them without ever noticing that the people they are talking to would rather watch paint dry than continue the conversation. This causes other children to avoid them.

Warning Sign #5: Takes Things the Wrong Way

They may explode over little things, cry for no reason, or just respond badly. Many children with disordered social skills take things the wrong way, and as a result they respond incorrectly.

Warning Sign #6: Getting into Trouble at School

Children who can't read social cues and do not know how to initiate or respond to social interactions will find themselves getting into trouble a lot. They usually do not understand why. For example, the teachers of one little boy I know told his parents he was sexually harassing a little girl when in fact he just did not understand personal space. How sad is that?

Warning Sign #7: They Just Don't Get It

What they don't get depends on the child, but it will fall within the six main areas of social language, which are:

1. **Poor command of conversation rules and topic maintenance.**

   a. **Some children can't start conversations.** They may not try to start them. They may become really uncomfortable and awkward when they do.

   b. **Some children don't understand how to have mutual focus.** That means they have trouble staying on topic and not veering off into topics that don't relate to the conversation at hand.

c. Some children don't understand the give and take, the back and forth. It may be they talk and talk without giving other people chances, or it may be they don't talk enough and force other people to keep the conversation going.

2. **Poor ability to read and use body language appropriately.**

    Research shows that most of our communication is nonverbal. We converse with facial expressions, gestures, and other forms of movement. We may step back when we feel other people are too close. They may step forward if they miss our signals. We may look at our watches or the door if we're in a hurry or bored. They may keep talking and talking if they miss the signals. There are an infinite number of nonverbal signals children can get wrong if they have trouble with nonverbal language (see chapter 6).

3. **Poor emotional control.**

    Some children get upset too easily. It may be they take things too personally or get frustrated and can't keep their emotions in check. A big part of navigating the social world is knowing when to express emotions and when to conceal them. There are even times when we need to show indifference when we're happy or seem happy when we're sad. When children have poor emotional control, they make easy targets for those who want to manipulate their emotions for their own enjoyment. This is one of the key tactics used by bullies (see chapter 8).

4. **Lack of understanding of how to act in different situations** (see chapter 4).

5. **Inability to take another person's perspective. No theory of mind** (see chapter 5).

FIGURE 3

The Most Important Social Milestones Your Child Should Be Reaching

There are specific social-skills milestones your child should reach. Here are some of the most important he or she should be reaching between the ages of one and fourteen. Please note this list is not meant to replace consulting with a professional.

By the age of one
Smiles spontaneously, responds to his own name, responds to no, responds differently to strangers than to familiar people, imitates simple actions of others

Between ages one and two
Refers to self by name, initiates self-play and will play alone, recognizes self in mirror or picture, imitates adult behaviors in play, helps put things away

Between ages two and three
Plays near other children, will watch them and briefly join in their play, begins pretend play, participates in simple group activity, knows gender identity, defends own positions, symbolically uses objects when playing

Between ages three and four
Joins in play with other children for longer periods and begins to interact, shares toys, takes turns with assistance, begins acting out whole scenes in dramatic play

Between ages four and five
Comfortably plays and interacts with other children, shows interest in exploring gender differences, has realistic dramatic play with specific details

Between ages five and six
Chooses own friends; plays competitive games; engages in cooperative play with other children involving group decisions, role assignments, and fair play

Between ages six and ten
Makes friends easily and friends become more important, knows right from wrong, needs love and understanding, becomes more self-aware and self-esteem can be fragile, becomes a better loser and more able to accept blame, feels guilt and shame, likes clubs and teams, wants to be part of a group

Between ages ten and fourteen
Establishes individuality and separation from parents; friends and social life become the primary motivations of behavior

For more information about social-skills disorders, visit www.WhereICanBeMe.com.

What You Can Do at Home

While there is no way to replace the personalized guidance of a qualified professional, there are some things you can do at home that can be immensely helpful to your child.

CHAPTER 8

Friend-Away

There are some behaviors that repel friendships if not kept in check. Here are the eight most common friendship repellents and how you can help.

Our children are special. To us they are perfect just the way they are. Of course nobody is perfect, including our children. As much as we love them, if we think about them objectively we can see the things about them that cause problems in their lives. We all have behaviors that can be bothersome to other people; that's okay. The world would be a dreary place if we were all the same. However, there are some behaviors that act as friendship repellents if not kept in check.

One of the first steps in helping your child is to look at him or her objectively and understand the things he or she is doing to repel friends. With that in mind, I will list eight friendship repellents, along with some tips on how you can help your child. However, as you read through them, it is important to keep in mind that you should not try to shove a square peg through a round hole. That means no matter what your child's personality is, your goal should not be to make your child like everyone else. Your goal should be to help your child learn to function effectively in the social world in which he or she lives. Sometimes that means controlling behaviors he or she has; other times it may require exhibiting behaviors with which your child is not particularly comfortable.

Friendship Repellent #1: Unaware

Unaware children miss or misinterpret the emotions and/or other social signals of their friends. It is very difficult to maintain friendships when this happens. Like most things unawareness exists on a spectrum. Some children are a little unaware. Some are totally unaware, and most are somewhere in between.

Many children who suffer socially tend to be somewhat unaware when it comes to the emotions of others; after all why would they continue to do things that cause problems socially if they were fully aware of what other people thought? So as we look at the other bad friendship behaviors, it is important to keep unawareness in mind. Problems with theory of mind and perspective taking (chapter 5) often play significant roles in this.

HOW TO HELP UNAWARENESS

If your child has difficulty in this area, you should talk about how other people are feeling in different situations. Try to help your child see things from other people's perspectives. Help your child understand how his or her words and actions impact other people. You should also seek professional guidance to determine if your child is having trouble with theory of mind and perspective taking.

Friendship Repellent #2: Too Emotional

These are the kids who let their emotions get the best of them. They may have tantrums or crying fits, or they may just shut down. Their most defining characteristic is that they are prone to reacting with too much emotion or with the wrong emotion altogether. These kids make easy targets for bullies since it's easy to get them to overreact.

HOW TO HELP YOUR CHILD MANAGE EMOTIONS

If this is a new development, you should look to see what is happening in your child's life. Is there something causing stress that needs to be dealt with? If so, taking care of that may solve the problem. Of course some children are more emotional by nature while others learn it from the people in their lives.

Whatever is going on, it is important to help your child learn to stay calm. Talk to your child, and help him or her learn to recognize what his or her own emotions are. Also help your child recognize when emotions are rising so he or she can better control them. Teach strategies for controlling emotions, and make sure to model good emotional control in your home. It will be hard to get your child to control his or her emotions if you or the other people in your home can't control their emotions. You should avoid engaging in emotional battles with your child. When you see things are starting to get emotional, disengage, and come back to the conversation later.

The ability to manage emotions is so important, and I have dedicated chapter 10 to this subject.

Friendship Repellent #3: Too Impulsive

Some kids have a very hard time controlling their impulses. I have a child who struggles with this. I can tell when she has a thought because it immediately manifests in either her behavior or words. These kids can come across as insensitive, obnoxious, and disrespectful.

HOW TO HELP IMPULSIVITY

Impulsive kids need help thinking things through. They also need help understanding how their actions affect others. The majority of these children are caring and do not want to hurt others. That is why helping them understand how their actions affect others can be very effective in helping them control their impulses. Participating in structured activities with guidance can also help them learn to control their impulses. However, it is important they still have unstructured time. This will provide an outlet for them to release their pent-up energy.

Impulsivity is related to emotional control, and you can learn more about how to help your impulsive child in chapter 10.

Friendship Repellent #4: Bossy

These children have to have things their way. They are rigid in their views of the world and try to control all outcomes. Others can see them as self-centered and overbearing.

HOW TO HELP BOSSINESS

As a parent you need to teach your child to appreciate the contributions of others. You also need to help your child channel his or her leadership capabilities. While there are times to be rigid and steadfast, there are also many times when it is important to be flexible. Chapter 9 is dedicated to helping children who struggle with flexibility.

Friendship Repellent #4: The Know-It-All

We all want our children to be smart, and being smart is a good thing. However, other people don't like to feel stupid. Know-it-all children tend to talk down to others, one-up others' stories, and take away others' glory. They may also talk about details in which other people are not interested.

HOW TO HELP A KNOW-IT-ALL

If your child likes to show off the depth and breadth of his or her knowledge, you may need to help dial it back. Sometimes this may mean letting other kids have the spotlight and not adding to what they are saying. Other times it may mean ignoring when they are wrong. This can be very confusing for a child since it might seem people would want to know what is right. Of course as an adult you know that is not the case, so you need to help them know when to display what they know and when to keep quiet. The trick is to do this without stifling their hunger for knowledge.

Friendship Repellent #5: Gossip

Good friends are trustworthy. Bad friends gossip. Good friends can keep secrets. Bad friends can't. Good friends stick up for each other. Bad friends talk behind your back.

HOW TO HELP A CHILD WHO GOSSIPS

If your child gossips, you need to teach him or her the good-friend rules and make sure you follow them yourself. Gossiping kids often have gossiping adults in their lives. So pay attention to how you talk about your friends and family members. You may be surprised by the example you are setting.

Friendship Repellent #6: Victim/Pessimistic

Have you ever had friends who were total downers? Sure you have. We all have at some point. They were the friends who seemed to have black clouds hanging over them, and it seemed justified because bad things always happened to them. They were a lot like the old Charlie Brown cartoons. Charlie Brown always complained and saw the worst in situations because he had a victim/pessimistic personality. Because of that he always managed to mess things up, create problems, and irritate his friends.

Some amount of pessimism can be a good thing because it can help kids avoid unnecessary risks. However, too much of it really turns off other people. Nobody likes to feel sad or think about bad things all the time.

HOW TO HELP A PESSIMISTIC CHILD

Help your child see the good in things and people. Most often even bad things are not as bad as they first seem, and how we view them is a choice. It can also help to let them know how other people view a negative attitude.

Friendship Repellent #7: Too Competitive

Competition is natural and a good thing. It is how we get better at things. We all like to win; however, some kids take it too far. They tend to be poor winners and even worse losers. They may gloat when they win and make excuses when they don't. In extreme cases they will lie, cheat, and steal to win. They make life miserable for the kids who are trying to have fun.

Sports and games are not the only things with which kids can be overcompetitive. It can happen with toys, clothes, appearances, houses, or just about anything else of which you can think. Children can be jealous of others. While some kids are super competitive by nature, there is often an underlying cause, such as a low self-esteem, a need for status, or trying to live up to the expectations of others.

HOW TO HELP AN OVERCOMPETITIVE CHILD

If your child is too competitive, the first thing you should do is consider how winning and losing is dealt with in your household. Is there a constant push for perfection? Does someone cheat to win or blame others when he or she loses? Does someone always gloat when he or she wins? Does someone behave badly when watching sports on TV? Is someone a sore loser? Does someone use his or her possessions as a barometer of status? If so that needs to be changed. Help your child have a healthy relationship with competition. Winning and losing are facts of life.

Sometimes behaviors are passed down through generations. Just like abuse, neglect, and substance abuse can be passed down, so too can negative social behaviors.

Friendship Repellent #8: Tattletale

Nobody likes a tattletale. On the other hand, sometimes it's necessary. A good rule of thumb is that if someone is in danger, it's a good time to tell an adult. If someone is just being annoying or doing something you disagree with, it's not a time to tell an adult. Too often kids use tattling as a way to get adults to solve their social problems.

HOW TO HELP A TATTLETALE

Teach your child how to solve his or her own social problems. There are some things he or she should just let go. There are some things he or she should try to stop, and there are some things from which he or she should just walk away. Teach your child the types of things for which he or she needs an adult. Teach your child the things for which he or she doesn't need an adult.

DON'T SOLVE YOUR CHILD'S PROBLEMS. HELP YOUR CHILD FIND THE SOLUTIONS.

No matter what type of child you have, it is easy to get caught up in the moment. We all want to save our children. It is difficult to watch them struggle. It is even more difficult to watch them fail. However, life is full of struggles and failure. Our job is not to shelter our children from these realities but to help them learn to overcome them.

We need to empower them to be successful. To do this we must slow down and think about what the problem really is. From there we need to help them discover the solutions. This can be extremely challenging to do, especially in today's hurried world. It is often easier either to do it for them or to tell them how to do it. However, it is important to help your child find the solution. One way to do this is by identifying the problem with your child and asking your child the next step to solve it. You may need to prompt your child with an idea, but always ask him or her the next step and gradually work your way through it. If your child has already failed at solving the problem, you need to ask, "What else could you do to make the outcome more positive?"

It can also help to talk about how you solve social problems in your life when they arise. While you shouldn't talk about every social problem that comes up and all the details, don't be afraid to talk about routine problems and the steps you are taking to solve them.

Above all make sure to model appropriate social skills. Children copy the behaviors of those around them, so make sure you are setting a good example.

CHAPTER 9

Flexibility

Addressing mental and social flexibility is often a key to success when helping children with social-skills disorders.

Flexibility is important. Although bones seem very hard, they are slightly flexible. If they weren't they would break more often than they do. The same goes for your child. While there are times to stand firm, there are other times when it is very important to be flexible. We touched on this in chapter 8 when discussing friendship repellents. However, this issue is so important, it needs its own chapter.

Many children who have trouble socially also have problems being flexible. Children who struggle with flexibility tend to see things in black and white. They often have trouble accepting the fact that rules change and occasionally need to be broken. They do not understand there is often a gray area.

WHY CHILDREN ARE INFLEXIBLE

Rules help many children understand the world around them. The rules can actually be calming to them. However, sometimes rules can get in the way. Many children have numerous rules they have developed for themselves and don't allow themselves to break. Children who struggle with theory of mind and perspective taking also tend to be inflexible since they have difficulty seeing things from other people's perspectives. They get hung up on their own ideas because of this. Whatever the cause, a lack of flexibility can be extremely frustrating to their families, their peers, and just about everyone else in their lives.

Addressing this lack of flexibility is often a key to success when helping children with social-skills disorders. Without addressing it, progress can't be made. Part of helping with flexibility is understanding that it plays an important role in everyone's life. There is a constant give and take in social situations. While rules give us order and let us know what to expect, there is a great deal of research that indicates the inability to think flexibly and adapt to current conditions is a big reason why many children and adults fail in education, work, and life. While rules are necessary, they can become hindrances if taken too far.

HOW DO WE ADDRESS THIS?

While teaching rules is essential, it is also essential to work on flexibility of thought. While there are steadfast rules, we need to teach children that everything is not always black and white. Often rules have gray areas. Something that might be okay in one environment might not be okay in another. For example, while it is perfectly okay to pass gas in the bathroom, it's not really okay to pass gas in class. Children need to learn that different places have different rules.

It is also important to let children know it is okay to break a rule if that is what it takes to stay safe. For instance, even though a teacher said not to leave the classroom unattended, it would be okay to leave if there were a fire. Another time it may be okay to break a rule is when it involves someone else's feelings. While it may be true that a person has bad breath, it is probably a bad idea to point that out unless you have a very close relationship with the person and do it discreetly. It is important to talk about this with your child and try to model flexible behavior yourself. Of course you don't want your child to be too flexible and let people take advantage of him or her.

This is a complicated topic. Everyone has different rules they live by. However, as we go through life, we often find that rules we thought were essential weren't, and rules we thought weren't were. While we don't want to teach our children to break rules, we want them to know that occasionally it is okay depending on circumstances. They need to understand that rules change based on circumstances, and they must be flexible and adapt.

CHAPTER 10

Self-Regulation

When self-regulation does not develop normally, a child will be at risk for many problems.

Many children who suffer from social-skills deficits have trouble with self-regulation. Normal self-regulation involves the ability to tolerate feelings of stress related to an unmet need, such as hunger, fatigue, or anxiety. The ability to self-regulate helps a child be less reactive and impulsive during times of challenge. In other words self-regulation is a child's ability to control his or her behavior in any given situation.

Many studies have shown that self-regulation is a predictor of academic success although it is not related whatsoever to intelligence. It is one of the most important milestones in life. Without the ability to self-regulate, functioning in any environment is extremely difficult.

SELF-REGULATION MILESTONES

Self-regulation develops over time. In infants up to six months, feelings of stress or discomfort are immediately addressed by a loving parent. Infants have no ability to self-regulate. After several months of their needs being met, they learn to wait just a bit by self-soothing. They may suck their hands or blankets to calm themselves until their needs are met. Babies who are better at self-soothing have stronger self-regulating abilities.

Ages One to Three

Young toddlers are just beginning to make connections between emotions and situations and are learning to connect emotions with their behaviors. They are now learning to change their behaviors when a parent asks. This ability is improving each day. During this stage an adult must be present or nearby. Most toddlers are extremely impulsive and can't be left alone for one minute. I once had a mother of a young toddler tell me that every time she put her child down and turned her back for a second, she felt like he was trying to kill himself. She was amazed by his lack of control over his behavior and his impulsivity. Fortunately, by the age of three, typically developing children will often behave in the way they think their mom or dad would want them to behave even without being watched. What a great stage for a parent to reach!

Ages Three to Five

The ability to connect emotion with behavior gets stronger in the three-to-five-year stage as children get ready for school environments. Some children will have the ability to self-regulate earlier, and some children older than five will still have difficulty with self-regulation.

DEVELOPING SELF-REGULATION

During the preschool stage, it is crucial to teach children to learn to wait. While they are learning to wait, we should label emotions to help children make the connection between the emotions and behaviors. Parents of preschoolers should also be very concrete when setting limits. This helps children learn what behaviors are acceptable and what behaviors are not. A child should always know what the expectations are in any given situation. By doing this we help children gain better control over their impulses and start to think more before they act.

Children with special needs may have delays and challenges when it comes to self-regulation. Some children may struggle with self-regulation and have no other special needs. When self-regulation does not develop normally, children will be at risk for many problems. Some of the difficulties they will have include the regulation of eating and sleeping.

I always ask about these topics when working with parents of children who I suspect are having difficulties with self-regulation. These children may also have persistent tantrums and impulsive behaviors that are obvious to the outside world. Sometimes parents miss these signs because they are so accustomed to their child's behavior, they think it is normal.

In order to improve a child's ability to self-regulate, we must challenge the child at low levels. When challenges are small and repetitive, children will slowly learn to tolerate stress and control their behaviors. Once this is accomplished, the level of challenge can be increased to the next level.

It is important not to overwhelm the child by moving too fast. The goal is not to overwhelm him or her, which carries the risk of the child shutting down. The goal is to change the behavior gradually over time so it becomes natural

This approach is part of the reason we see amazing progress with children who join our social-skills program to help with self-regulation. Our environment is structured and predictable, and so we are able to challenge the children behaviorally in small doses and increase the challenges as needed.

One boy who started our class at age six would yell, scream, and cry and actually tried to climb the walls when he first joined. One year later he was a different child. He was able to wait for his favorite activities as well as greet and share with his friends. It was beautiful to see and very rewarding to everyone who worked with him!

I know it can be exhausting to live with a child who has self-regulation issues. However, it is important to remember who your child is and what he or she can handle. Try to set your child up for success and not for failure. Turn down invitations to events you know he or she can't handle, and try to keep as much of your child's typical routine in place as you can during holidays, vacations, and school breaks.

Most importantly don't decrease your expectations for behavior during these breaks. Even though you may think you are being nice by loosening the rules, you are likely making it harder on your child. The more consistent you are, the easier it will be for everyone when the time comes to transition back into school.

Last but certainly not least, don't be afraid to seek professional guidance if you feel your child is struggling with self-regulation. It is much easier and less frustrating to help a child develop this critical life skill with the guidance of a qualified expert than it is alone.

As parents we are so emotionally involved, it is hard to make the right choices and handle these situations effectively. Even though I am a therapist, sometimes I have to take a step back when dealing with the behavioral challenges of my own children. I often ask myself, "What would I do as a therapist?" Sometimes I even ask my colleagues for their opinions. I can tell you from experience, it helps to get assistance from professionals who are not emotionally attached to the situation.

CHAPTER 11

Play

Through play, children learn how to negotiate, share, resolve conflicts, and make decisions.

In our constant drive toward achievement and learning as a society, we have forgotten the most important way in which children learn, the way in which they discover themselves and build relationships with others: play. Some scientists think play is as important as sleep and food. In fact this view is so widespread, even the United Nations recognizes play as a right of every child.

Far from being mindless and silly, play is critical to childhood development. Studies show that through play, children learn many things, including how to negotiate, share, resolve conflicts, and make decisions. It also helps children relieve stress and energy while improving physical ability and health. Play helps children develop their imaginations as well as their cognitive and social abilities. Play also helps children strengthen emotional bonds with those they play with, including their parents.

While studies show play has a positive effect on a child's development, studies also show a lack of play can be detrimental. According to a 1997 article in *Time* magazine titled "Fertile Minds," research conducted at Baylor College of Medicine indicated children who don't develop imagination through spontaneous play have brains 20 to 30 percent smaller than children of the same age who do play.

There is also a growing body of evidence showing a lack of play is contributing to higher levels of stress, anxiety, depression, and anger, along with lower levels of coping skills and imagination in today's children. It seems many of the problems we see in children and young adults are originating in over-structured childhoods that don't give children the opportunity to play.

WHAT IS PLAY?

In this instance we're talking about what's referred to as *free play*. It can be simple word games, pretend play, tag, jumping rope, or even something the child makes up, but it is not video games. This is especially true for children who struggle socially. Video games are not social by nature. Even multiplayer and virtual-reality games are no substitute for imaginative and interactive play. When it comes to play, it is important for children to interact with others and use their imaginations and their physical abilities.

Think about playing a game of Simon Says. What does it take to be successful at it? Simon needs to come up with creative directions to try to stump the other players, who need to be able to concentrate, follow directions, and control impulses because "Simon" is trying to trick them into doing the wrong thing.

Now think about Freeze Tag. What does it take to be successful? While it doesn't take the same impulse control and concentration as Simon Says, it does require stamina, strategy, and anticipating the decisions of others. In the game you have one child or team who is "it." In order to win, whoever is it must freeze all the other players by tagging them. Each of the other children needs to avoid being the last person frozen so he or she doesn't become it in the next round. The players who are not frozen can unfreeze their teammates in order to keep the game going and reduce the risk of being tagged last; however, they must avoid being tagged in the process. That means it takes strategy to win and in the case of the runners, cooperative teamwork.

These are just two examples of countless games children play and some of the skills they learn in the process. Not only are they far from being mindless, but these childhood games are also critical for our children's development. While it is not necessary to play outside, it is ideal because exposure to natural settings is shown to help children handle stress better, concentrate better, and have improved impulse control and less aggression.

THE DEATH OF PLAY

Unfortunately children spend far less time outside participating in unstructured play today than they did in generations past. Today most parents work and have less time. They and their children are also overwhelmed with homework and distracted by an endless array of electronic gadgets and games.

Play is also very limited at school. Usually the students have one short outside recess if they are lucky. Even that may not last since there are people pushing to start structuring play during recess as well. While more and more scientific evidence is building in favor of play, and many more people are advocating for recess, the tide is still moving in favor of less play and more work in schools. That means it is up to us to find the time to get our children outside and playing.

Playdates are one option. However, it is important to keep in mind that children who have trouble socially can't pick up on social cues in the same way typical children do, so you need to make sure you invite children with similar social skills and interests as your child. This will help make the playdate a success. I have included ten tips for successful playdates at the end of this chapter.

WHAT YOU LEARN FROM PLAY

You should set aside time to play with your kids both alone and when they have friends over. I don't know about you, but it's hard for me to engage my children unless I turn off my gadgets. So turn off yours, leave them inside, and embrace your inner child. It will be good for both of you. Playing with your child can open up a whole new perspective. What better way to get an understanding of how your child thinks and feels than by playing with him or her? Play lets children be themselves, and it allows them to pursue the things that interest them.

Through play children show how they think and make decisions. Their actions and their words will teach you a lot about what's on their minds. You will also be able to see some of the reasons they have trouble socially. Some of this will come from observation, and some of it will come from what they tell you as you play.

Play will also allow you to help your child in a subtle, nonthreatening, and noncritical way because you can do it within the context of playing a game. Play will allow you to build a better relationship with your child and might even make you feel just a bit younger. Don't you miss the carefree days of playing with your friends when you were a child? All it takes to feel that again is letting go and embracing your child in the moment. So send your child outside, let him or her get dirty, and don't be afraid to join in. It is not a waste of time; it is some of the most important time you'll ever spend with your child.

FIGURE 4

Ten Tips for Successful Playdates

1. Start off with very short playdates.
I would not recommend any longer than one hour. Thirty to forty-five minutes would be ideal. This will reduce the risk of problems and put less pressure on everyone. You can always gradually increase the length of time for later playdates.

2. Have the playdate at your house.
This will eliminate the stress of a new environment for your child. You will want to make sure he or she is ready before sending him or her to play at other children's homes.

3. Get input from your child.
Find out who he or she would want to invite over to play. It doesn't make sense to invite a child your child doesn't want to come over.

4. Invite only one other child.
Three children will not play as well as two children. Inevitably one child will be left out. This may or may not bother the child with special needs, but it does defeat the purpose of the playdate if he or she is the one left out.

5. Have repetitive playdates with the same child.
This will allow the children to develop a relationship with each other.

6. Keep siblings out of the room.
I know from experience that this is easier said than done. However, this is important if your child is struggling socially. If the sibling is unwilling to stay out of the room, it may be a good time to arrange for him or her to be at someone else's house for a play-date or with a family member.

7. Talk to your child about sharing before the playdate.
Prior to the playdate, allow him or her to put away any toys he or she does not want to share.

8. Don't worry about "perfect."
Things will go wrong. They always do. Worrying about making everything perfect puts way too much pressure on you, your child, and the potential new friend.

9. Playdates should be supervised but not micromanaged.
The age and functioning levels of the children should determine the level of supervision. Older children with adequate language skills may require only occasional adult assistance while younger children with

developmental delays may initially require constant adult facilitation. When problems arise try to let the kids work them out. If they can't, help them see the steps to work them out, but resist solving the problems for them.

10. Get expert help if needed.

Sometimes it is better to bring in a professional who has experience managing playdates for children who struggle socially. Speech-language pathologists are excellent choices for playdate facilitation. This is because playdate problems typically arise when one or both of the children are lacking appropriate communication skills. A good facilitator can do wonders as far as taking the pressure off you and helping your child learn to navigate social situations appropriately.

It is also important to keep in mind that if your child has a true social-skills disorder, you will need to find a reputable social-skills group to help your child learn the skills he or she is unable to pick up without intervention.

❧

Getting Help from Professionals

❧

When a child is struggling socially, professional guidance is often necessary. Unfortunately, finding someone who can actually help is an extremely difficult task.

CHAPTER 12

The Right Help

Most people claiming to teach social skills don't actually know what they are doing.

Considering the importance of social skills in many areas of our lives, it is a very good thing that they can be taught. The problem is they can't be taught by just anybody. They must be taught by someone who knows what he or she is doing. Unfortunately, most people claiming to teach social skills don't actually know what they are doing. Most don't have any training or even a rudimentary understanding of what social skills really are. It is very much a case where the buyer needs to beware.

Anyone can claim to help your child develop social skills. If you have picked up any parenting magazine or watched any kids' shows, you know what I am talking about. Ads for everything from gymnastics schools to cartoons are claiming they can teach your child social skills. It is the buzzword of the day.

In fairness, for a typically developing child who is learning through observation and exposure, those programs may work to some degree; however, these programs do not work for children who have true social-skills disorders. Remember, children with social-skills disorders struggle to learn these skills without being directly taught by a competent professional. That is why picking the right social-skills group is absolutely necessary and extremely important if you want to help your child.

When it comes to social-skills groups, and any type of therapy, for that matter, something is not always better than nothing. I can't count how many frustrated parents have come to me after wasting time and money with several different programs claiming to develop social skills. In the best-case scenarios, the children had fun in the programs but did not improve their social skills. In the worst cases, the programs were actually harmful because they set the children back and made them resistant to therapy. That is why you want to do everything in your power to make sure you don't join the wrong group.

Forming social-skills groups is the hardest thing I have ever done. They are logistical nightmares. You need to find the right kids and get them in the right place at the same time with the right therapist to make them work. However, when they do work, they are great!

Because there is such a high demand for these groups and because they are so difficult to put together correctly, you need to be aware of people who are desperate to start groups and will place your child in the wrong class. While I don't have a foolproof way for you to avoid bad programs, I do have seven rules and six key questions that will help you avoid wasting time and money.

THE SEVEN RULES FOR GETTING THE RIGHT HELP.

Rule #1: Research All the Different Groups You Can Find

Visit their websites, and request their printed materials. Ask other people about the experiences they've had with different groups. Even if you don't personally know someone whose child needed social-skills therapy, someone you know does. Ask your friends. Ask your pediatrician and your child's teachers. See if you can find mommy or daddy groups either online or in your community that you can ask. Find out what their personal experiences were like. Use that to narrow down your list of potential programs. Reputation isn't a guarantee, but it is generally a good indicator.

Rule #2: Don't Join a Group without First Having an Enrollment Consultation

Remember, it is a good thing when a program requires a consultation before you can join. It is a necessary step. They have to meet your child and get to know what his or her strengths and needs are. While you can learn some things about the program and the director can learn some things about your child on the phone, there is no way to make a proper placement without a professional meeting your child in person for an enrollment consultation. A phone call won't let you get a good feel for the program either.

When you go to your enrollment consultation, you should be prepared to speak honestly and openly with the evaluator. You should also keep an open mind. Sometimes the evaluator and the parents will see a child's strengths and weaknesses somewhat differently. That's okay. The important thing is to have an open, honest, and respectful discussion about how to help your child.

If after the consultation you believe the program is a good fit, you can keep it on your list of possibilities. If you don't think it is going to be a good fit, then you should move on to a different program.

Rule #3: Make Sure You Have at Least Four Weeks to Try Classes without Risking Your Money

Placement will be crucial to your child's success. Think of the Goldilocks Principle: you don't want the kids to be too advanced or too delayed—you want them to be just right.

A reputable program knows that even with a stringent placement process, sometimes they will get the placement wrong. It often takes a few weeks to tell how a placement is going to work out. That is why you shouldn't have to risk your money during that time. If a placement fails within that timeframe, you should either get your money back or have it applied to a different group within the program.

Rule #4: Don't Join a Program Just Because It Has a Convenient Timeslot

Good social-skills programs are in high demand, and proper placement is difficult. That means there is a high probability your child will have to spend some amount of time on a waiting list before the right spot opens up. That's okay. It is better to wait for the right placement than to waste time and money on the wrong placement.

Rule #5: Don't Use Price as Your Primary Guide

Not all social-skills programs are created equal. You cannot expect programs on the low end of the price spectrum to have the same quality of service as those on the high end of the spectrum. Of course a high price does not guarantee quality either.

You should consider price to be a signal of the kind of quality you will receive. It is only one piece of the puzzle. You need to look deeper to make sure the program will be a good fit for your child.

While the price will need to fit your budget, please remember that something is not better than nothing. The wrong program can set your child back and make him or her resistant to therapy. I see this often. If your child needs help, the quality of the social-skills program should be a top priority in your budget.

Rule #6: Don't Use Location as Your Primary Guide

Good social-skills programs are few and far between. That's why it always surprises me when I hear of a parent insisting on a program that is "no more than ten minutes away." That is not a reasonable expectation for most people. Even here in the New York tri-state area, many parents find themselves driving over an hour each way several times a week for therapy. While those who do so are exceptions, a lot of the families who come to my office drive between twenty and forty minutes each way.

Rule #7: Follow Your Intuition

This last step is true of everything we do as parents. You have to listen to your gut. Sometimes everything looks great on paper, but something just doesn't feel right. I had a personal experience when my seven-month-old son had torticollis and was getting physical therapy. Our first therapist came very highly recommended as being the best for babies with torticollis. Unfortunately, the whole experience was miserable for us. I walked out of each session feeling worse than the week before. We stuck with it for a few months until I realized I was doing what I tell parents not to do. Aaron was not getting anything positive from the sessions. What's worse is that he was getting more and more resistant to therapy. So I made a switch, and I am so happy I did. The difference was like night and day. The experience with the new therapist was positive, and we achieved our goals with smiles on our faces.

A social-skills group should be fun for your child. If your child is miserable in a group, he or she should not be forced to attend because it will not help. Aside from wasting time, it may make your child resistant to a program that is a better fit. Children and adults want to replicate positive, successful social interactions. Socializing is supposed to be fun. While there must also be an appropriate learning component, your child needs to enjoy the program or it will not be useful. When kids are having fun together, they often do not realize they are learning important social skills.

That's not to say you should pull your child out of a group if he or she doesn't have fun at first. Sometimes it does take a child a little while to warm up to the other kids. You should give it at least until the end of the trial/guarantee period. Don't fall into the trap of bouncing around from group to group without ever giving any group a chance.

THE SIX KEY QUESTIONS YOU MUST ASK ANY SOCIAL-SKILLS GROUP BEFORE JOINING

In the time I have been forming and running social-skills groups, I have learned a lot about what is important for parents to know and look for and what questions you should be asking to make sure a class is the right fit for your child.

Like I always say, no therapist or group is the right fit for every child even though some may claim to be. You need to find a program and group that matches your child's needs and personality. The following six questions will help you to do that.

Must-Ask Question #1: Who Is Running the class?

As I have said before, it seems like everyone has started claiming they can teach social skills. The problems is that the vast majority of those claiming they can teach these skills have absolutely no training or qualifications to do so. That's why the first step is to figure out the qualifications of the person running the class.

Children with true social-skills disorders, which are actually pragmatic-language disorders (remember, pragmatic language is the social use of language), need someone who is an expert in pragmatic language. That is why my groups are run by speech-language pathologists who specialize in pragmatic language. I like to use the example that you would not go to anyone other than a dentist for a toothache, so why would you go to anyone other than a speech-language pathologist for a pragmatic-language disorder? Another reason a speech-language pathologist is typically the best choice is these children often have other language deficits as well. The other language deficits may be subtle, but they are typically there.

Now, if the child's main issue is an emotional or behavioral issue, our group is likely not the right fit. A social worker or a psychologist would be better. So a child with pure oppositional defiant disorder or schizophrenia would not be appropriate for our classes. However, it is important to remember that many behavioral issues are caused by a child's difficulties with social skills. A child who does not know how to interact appropriately with others might find himself or herself in trouble a lot.

Sometimes, however, behavior problems are not due to social skills. For example, I once had a child who was sneaking razor blades into school come in for a consultation. This child was not the right fit for my groups, which are run by speech-language pathologists. That is why this child was immediately referred to a psychologist who runs social-skills groups for children with true emotional and/or behavioral problems.

Sometimes behavior problems and pragmatic-language disorders coexist. When this happens it is often best for a speech-language pathologist and a behavior expert such as a clinical psychologist to work together to address both issues simultaneously.

Must-Ask Question #2: How Are the Children Placed?

Placement in the proper group is critically important and difficult. That is why you need to ask a lot of questions about how children are placed. It is not something that can be done without an evaluator meeting your child. It could be the director or one of the therapists who runs the groups. The important thing is that they have the qualifications to evaluate your child's skills and can determine if one of the groups in the program is a good fit. I know I have said it before, but you need to beware of anyone who asks your child's age and diagnosis and places him or her in a class without first meeting your child. That is a clear sign this person does not know what he or she is doing. You can't just throw a bunch of kids together and expect it to work.

While age and diagnosis are factors in placement, your child's strengths, needs, and personality are much more important. Aside from helping the function and progress of the group, appropriate placement also helps to make sure each child will have at least one or two potential peers in the group who could become his or her friends. This cannot be determined without an initial consultation that assesses each child's strengths, needs, and personality.

Must-Ask Question #3: What Is the Class Model? How Is It Run?

A program may use a direct model, an indirect model, or a blend of both for teaching social skills.

A purely indirect model will model behavior but will not specifically state what is being taught. For example, a therapist may model age-appropriate social interactions within a small group with the goal of having the children in the group imitate these social skills. This model is not appropriate for children who have social-skills disorders because they can't learn from modeling alone.

A purely direct model of teaching is like a sitting in a lecture. The therapist will talk about the skill and how to apply it without actually modeling the behavior in real situations. The problem with this model is that while children learn what to do from it, they do not learn how to use the skills. This is why many children can't carry over the skills they learn from this type of program into their everyday lives.

Blended models bring together elements of both direct and indirect teaching. When done correctly they replicate natural situations that allow the children to practice the skills they learn. The skills should become progressively more complex as the children gain ability and social sophistication. I have found this approach is the most useful in teaching social skills.

Must-Ask Question #4: What Is the Size of the Class?

The needs of the class will have an effect on the maximum size it should be. You want to look for a class that has six kids or fewer. Even with kids who are just a little "quirky," groups that are bigger than six are difficult to manage and maintain. The tendency is for kids, especially the quieter ones, to get lost in the shuffle and get overshadowed by the louder ones. A group of six should have at least one therapist and one assistant. Sometimes it will need a therapist and two assistants. But it should never have fewer than one therapist and one assistant.

For children with more-significant needs, a smaller group is more appropriate. However, in most instances I would not suggest having fewer than three kids in a group.

Having only two kids in a group, which is called a *dyad*, tends to put too much pressure on the kids to like each other. It also puts a lot of pressure on the parents. What if one child tells his parent he does not like the other child and does not want to come back? It feels too much like a blind date to me. Other professionals might feel differently; however, that is my opinion on dyads and something for you to keep in mind.

What size group your child needs will be determined by an enrollment consultation. When in doubt, I believe, it is better to start with a smaller group. Once the goals are addressed there, skills can be carried over into a larger group. That is an easy and natural progression.

Starting with a smaller group and then moving to a larger group will also help the therapist see if there are any other concerns, such as anxiety, that may need to be addressed before moving into the larger group.

Must-Ask Question #5: How Does the Program Help Parents with Carryover?

It always surprises me when parents tell me stories about being in other programs and having no idea what goes on, what the goals are, and what they could be doing for carryover.

Before you sign your child up for a social-skills program, you need to ask what the therapist will do to help your child take the skills he or she learns in class and then transfer them into his or her everyday life. This is a critical piece of a good social-skills program and not an easy thing to do. Unfortunately most groups either do not do it or do not do it correctly. So you need to ask before you join.

You should get a good deal of homework and have ongoing consultations with the therapist to help set and measure goals. The therapist needs to consult with you and the other professionals in your child's life, such as teachers at the very least. The more assistance you can get outside the group the better. Utilize playdate facilitation, and have the therapist help your child in real-life social situations, even at parties.

These types of carryover and involvement are incredibly important to your child's success. The goal should always be for your child to be able to use his or her new skills in his or her everyday life, not just in the group. It is something you should stay on top of even if the therapist gives you things to work on at home. Ask the therapist what else you can be doing. The more involved and proactive you are, the more involved and proactive your therapist will be. Show interest, and be engaged.

Must-Ask Question #6: What Is the Policy about Socializing out of Class?

As odd as it may seem, many programs actually frown upon children getting together outside the group. That doesn't make any sense to me. The whole point of a social-skills program is to help children develop their abilities to make friends and manage relationships. So what good is a social-skills program that says the members can't be friends?

Friendships help the children develop social skills. Friendships also help the parents. They give parents opportunities to have support from other people who are having similar experiences with their own children. All these parents have children who struggle socially, and if the placement has been done correctly, they should all have children who are good peers for one another. That is why I feel very strongly that these friendships should be encouraged.

We actually got noise complaints because of one group of dads. They were laughing and joking during their Tuesday Night Man Club, as they called it. They were having a big old time. Their voices really carried throughout the whole building. While the other tenants didn't appreciate it, to me that's how the waiting room should be when kids are in a social-skills group. Everyone should have fun. Everyone should become friends—not just the kids but the parents too. That's not to say they have to be friends outside the program, but I think it's a good thing when they are, and it should be encouraged.

CHAPTER 13

Not Helping

Reasons Why Children Fail to Make
Progress in Social-Skills Classes.

When thinking about social skills, an important point to keep in mind is that they evolve. What is expected of a child will change as he or she grows and changes. What a five-year-old knows and understands is much different from what an eleven-year-old should understand. However, when a child has trouble with social skills, the treatment should not be defined by his or her age.

Unfortunately this is a mistake I often see made even by therapists who should know better. Many times when reading goals and reports on children who struggle socially, I find the goals are much too advanced. They usually talk about a child having conversations when they should be talking about building foundational skills.

This is what happens when goals are based on the child's age and not his or her ability. The problem is if a child does not have the necessary social foundations, he or she will never be able to progress and carry over newly learned skills. This is not that different from most other areas of life. For example, if you can't hold a baseball bat correctly, you probably will not hit any home runs in the near future. So it does not make sense to practice putting power into your swing if you can't hold the bat right. It is the same when it comes to social skills. It doesn't make sense to teach a child advanced skills when he or she doesn't have the foundational skills.

FOUNDATIONAL SKILLS

One of the most important foundational skills a child will develop early on is joint attention. If a child has joint attention by the age of four, it is a positive sign of his or her prognosis. Joint attention is the process of sharing the experience of observing an object or event by following a gaze or pointing. For example, if your child sees something, looks at you as if to say, "Do you see what I see?" and then looks back at the thing, that is joint attention. Or if you point to something and your child looks to see what you are pointing at, that is also joint attention.

Joint attention is critical for social development. Typically developing children will acquire this skill as early as nine months. While joint attention seems simple, it is actually more complex than you would think. It involves paying attention to the outside world and the actions of people while at the same time paying attention to yourself. Without joint attention there would be no imitation. Without imitation there would be no language.

The next important foundational social skill involves emotional sharing and reciprocity. This refers to the ability to share emotions together. It is feeling as opposed to thinking. It involves enjoying an activity with someone else and being aware of it. Without this ability more-complex social interactions will not develop. This skill is necessary for being able to have a true friend.

The final foundational skills are perspective taking and theory of mind. Being able to understand others' intentions and take on their perspectives is crucial to social learning and building successful relationships. Individuals who do not have theory of mind and are unable to take others' perspectives are significantly impaired. When children do not have these skills, their relationships lack reciprocity, and there is little emotional sharing, as mentioned above. Empathy may also be lacking due to the inability to take someone else's perspective, which again leads to extreme difficulty forming close relationships.

As you can see, there is a lot more to social skills than having conversations, making eye contact, or simply knowing the rules. Social foundations must be in place for conversations to happen and for there to be any carryover of social skills into your child's daily life. Failing to build these foundational social skills is a big reason why a review of fifty-five school-based social-skills programs found they are minimally effective.

MORE REASONS FOR FAILURE

Another reason for their failures was that social goals were too broad. This speaks a lot to the competency of the therapist and the quality of the program. Unfortunately social-skills treatment is a relatively new area. It is totally unregulated, and the use of best practices is not widespread even among those who are technically qualified to treat social-skills disorders.

❦

Finding Your Way

❦

Nothing is more important to a child's development than a calm, loving, well-informed, and proactive parent. Without you nothing happens.

CHAPTER 14

Not Hopeless

---

*Every child has strengths, often
profound strengths, and it is
important that we recognize them.*

As you go on this journey with your child, it is important to remember that the diversity of life is what makes it interesting. The diversity of ideas is how we progress. Differences are important. Of course that doesn't stop humanity from shunning the deviations of ideas and nature. We've all heard how Galileo was treated for his views about the earth revolving around the sun at a time during which the opposite was believed to be true.

Today we have a culture that paradoxically promotes diversity while shunning children who have ADHD, autism, or any other disorder. While we have made great advancements from the widespread and horrific treatment of past decades, our society still focuses on what is "wrong" as opposed to what is "right."

Interestingly the determination of what is wrong and what is right has a lot to do with the time and place in which you live. What might be considered a gift in one culture may be considered a curse in another. This is not a new revelation. It goes back at least to 1975 when the former president of the American Psychological Association, Nicholas Hobbs, pointed it out in his book *The Futures of Children*. He observed that children are labeled to protect the society in which they live. In other words society, not nature, is making the determination about what is right or wrong.

This is important to keep in mind. The traditional model of health defines people by what they can't do as opposed to what they can do. It defines them by what is perceived to be wrong instead of what is right. "He's hyper." "She's depressed." "He can't communicate with us." As we focus on the things our culture tells us is wrong with these children, we often miss what makes them special. It may be that the child with ADHD is intensely creative and able to think of solutions others can't. It may be that the nonverbal child is able to see details everyone else misses. It may be something else entirely, but the reality is every child has strengths, often profound strengths, and it is important that we recognize them.

We also need to consider the environments that bring out the best and the worst in our children. Often the success or failure of a person with a given disorder is entirely dependent on the environment in which he or she finds himself or herself. No school is right for every child. No program is right for every child. No therapist is right for every child. No approach is right for every child. Each child is unique, and that is a very good thing.

This concept should be familiar to anyone who has heard me speak, read my writings elsewhere, or seen the name of my social-skills program, Where I Can Be Me®. I am a very strong advocate of creating environments that allow children to become their best selves. While that can be a difficult task at times, it is a necessary task. Allowing children to be true to themselves is critical to their well-being.

Too many therapy approaches focus on what is "wrong" and try to make a square peg become round. There is no right way to shove a square peg through a round hole. All that does is break off the edges. When this happens we lose something important.

That's not to say you should ignore your child's needs. It is simply to say you should not lose sight of your child's strengths. While you want your child to develop the skills to navigate the social world we live in, you don't want to take away his or her special talents; you want to add to them so your child can unlock his or her potential.

In the end your child's success depends on you and the decisions you make. You will make the choice to go through the steps I outlined or not. You will choose to stick with it or not. You will choose to carry over what your child is learning in the program or not. You will choose to be your child's guide in this or not.

I know this puts a tremendous amount of pressure on you, but the fact that you made it to this point in this book says a lot about the type of parent you are and the types of choices you are going to make for your child. No, your decisions will not be perfect. However, as you keep researching and keep engaging with those who are working to help your child, your decisions will get better. You and your child will get through this, and you will both be better because of it.

Made in the USA
Charleston, SC
13 September 2014